VEGAN REV' DEIT RECIPES

The Twenty-Two Vegan Challenge: 50 Healthy and Delicious Vegan Diet Recipes to Help You Lose Weight and Look Amazing

By
Tom Smith

Copyright © 2019 by: Tom Smith

ISBN-13: 978-1-950772-48-3
ISBN-10: 1-950772-48-9

All Rights Reserved. No part of this publication may be reproduced in any form or by any means, including scanning, photocopying, or otherwise without prior written permission of the copyright holder.

Disclaimer:

The information provided in this book is designed to provide helpful information on the subjects discussed. The publisher and author are not responsible for any specific health or allergy needs that may require medical supervision and are not liable for any damages or negative consequences from any treatment, action, application or preparation, to any person reading or following the information in this book.

VEGAN REV' DEIT RECIPES

Table of Contents

INTRODUCTION: 6

THE 22 DAY VEGAN SMOOTHIE TO HELP TRANSFORM YOUR BODY, RESET YOUR HABIT, AND CHANGE YOUR LIFE 7

    Scrambled Eggs with Avocado, Onion and Cheddar 7

    Edamame Salad with Avocado and Radishes 8

    Avocado and Chickpea Salad Sandwiches 10

    Vegan Twist on the Classic Tuna Sandwich 11

    Spinach and Avocado Salad with Garlic Mustard Vinaigrette 12

    Mango Avocado Salad 13

    Avocado and Cucumber Salad with Cilantro-Ginger Dressing 14

    Tuscan White Bean Soup 15

    Savory Bite-Sized Quinoa and Kale Patties 17

    Warm Wheat Berry Salad with Mushrooms and White Wine 19

    Lentil Salad with Lemon-Rosemary Vinaigrette 20

    Mushroom soup with White Beans 22

    Roasted Brussels sprouts with Orange Butter Sauce 23

    Chickpeas Simmered in Masala Sauce 25

    Braised Coconut Spinach with Chickpeas and Lemon 27

    Fingerling Potato Salad with Green Chili-Cilantro Salsa 29

    Five-minute vegan pancake 30

    Baja Black Beans, Corn and Rice 31

    Roasted Cauliflower & 16 Roasted Cloves of Garlic 32

    Roasted Green Beans 33

    Good Vegetarian Meatloaf (Really!) 34

    Sweet Cornbread 36

    Vegetarian Lasagna 37

    Vegetarian Chili 38

VEGAN REV' DEIT RECIPES

- Vegetarian Tacos 39
- Vegetarian "meatballs" 41
- Vegetarian Split Pea Soup 42
- Vegetarian Taco Soup 44
- Best Vegetarian Pot Stickers 46
- Uncle Bill's Vegetarian Minestrone Soup 48
- Vegetarian BLT 50
- Vegetarian Paella 51
- Southwest Vegetarian Bake 53
- Vegetarian Black Bean Soup 54
- Garbanzo Vegetarian Burgers 56
- Creamy Tortilla Soup-Vegetarian 57
- Vegetarian Apple Stir-Fry 58
- Vegetarian Taco Salad - Low Fat 59
- Very Quick Butter Chickpeas (Vegetarian Butter Chicken!) 60
- Fabulous Vegetarian Chili 61
- Oven Fried Eggplant (Aubergine) 63
- Roasted Brussels sprouts 64
- Greek Potatoes (Oven-Roasted and Delicious!) 65
- Hearty Vegetarian Tofu Chili 66
- Soy Glazed Tofu and Asparagus 67
- Tofu Egg Salad 68
- Marinated Baked Tofu 69
- Vegetarian Five Spice Tofu Stir-Fry 70
- Tibetan Greens with Tofu (Tse Tofu) 71
- Cauliflower with Salsa Verde 72
- Spicy Mushroom Stir-Fry 74
- Hearty Lentil Soup with Tomatoes 75
- Hot and Spicy Curried Tofu Scramble 77

- Spicy Roasted Cauliflower with Lemon 78
- Carrot and celeriac root salad with lemon sauce [Vegan] 79
- Hearty Vegetable Soup with Pasta Shells 80
- Cucumber Salad with Honey-Lime Yogurt Dressing 81
- Swiss chard and Goat Cheese Casserole 82
- Roasted Cauliflower with Olives and Rosemary 84
- Quick Homemade Gluten 85
- Scitan and Shiitake Mushroom Stroganoff 86
- Seitan Fusion Sauté 88
- Barbecued Seitan 90
- Seitan-Squash Sauté 91
- Mock BBQ Pork 93
- **CONCLUSION** 94

INTRODUCTION:
THE 22 DAY VEGAN CHALLENGE: TRANSFORM YOUR BODY, RESET YOUR HABIT, AND CHANGE YOUR LIFE

The vegan revolution is a groundbreaking program designed to transform your mental, emotional, and physical health in just 22 days.

The 22-Day vegan Revolution is founded on the principle that it takes 21 days to make or break a habit. *It* is also a plant-based diet designed to create lifelong habits that will empower you to live healthier, lose weight, or to reverse serious health issues. it benefits of a vegan diet are immense, most of which are: help prevent cancer, lower cholesterol levels, reduce the risk of heart disease, decrease blood pressure, and even reverse diabetes.

Marco Borges one of today's most sought-after health experts, exercise physiologist has spent years helping his exclusive list of high-profile clients to permanently change their lifestyle and bodies through his 22-day vegan revolution. Celebrities whose life has been touch with Marco Borges recent innovation ranges from Beyoncé, Jay-Z, Jennifer Lopez, and Pharrell Williams, to Gloria Estefan, and Shakira which have all turned to him for his expertise.

Diet and exercise are the building blocks for a healthy life, and Tom Smith when writing this book understands not only the scientific benefits to the human body, but also how to present the information in a way that is accessible, manageable, and inspirational. However, a plant-based diet can and will change your lifestyle for good. In *The vegan revolution diet recipes* will show you the best vegan smoothies for a trim waistline, a strong heart, and a healthy brain.

However, the 22 Days Nutrition is founded on the ground that vegan meals are the healthiest meals you can eat. Vegan meals are known to be low in calories and packed with vitamins and nutrients that are essential to the body. So while taking the 22 Days Nutrition diet, expect to eat between 1200 to 2000 calories per day even when you're eating regular meals and snacks. Vegan food is exceptionally low in calories.

Finally, this book contains "healthy and delicious" vegan recipes that anyone can use to break their bad dietary habits and start living a healthier life.

THE 22 DAY VEGAN SMOOTHIE TO HELP TRANSFORM YOUR BODY, RESET YOUR HABIT, AND CHANGE YOUR LIFE

Scrambled Eggs with Avocado, Onion and Cheddar

INGREDIENTS:

1 firm-ripe California avocado

1 1/3 cups of grated extra-sharp Cheddar (about 4 ounces)

2 small onion

8 large eggs

4 teaspoons of unsalted butter

Chopped fresh cilantro sprigs for garnish

Directions:

1. First, you chop onion, halve, pit, and peel avocado and cut into 1/4-inch pieces.
2. After which you whisk together eggs and Cheddar in a bowl.
3. After that, you season with salt and pepper.
4. At this point, you heat butter in a nonstick skillet over moderately high heat until foam subsides and sauté onion, stirring, about 2 minutes until just beginning to soften.
5. Then you add egg mixture and cook, stirring constantly, for about 1 minute until eggs are just set.
6. Furthermore, you remove skillet from heat and stir in avocado.
7. Finally, you serve eggs garnished with cilantro.

Edamame Salad with Avocado and Radishes

Ingredients

2 cloves of garlic (minced)

4 teaspoons of honey (**NOTE**: if you do not eat honey, I suggest you substitute with cane sugar or agave)

4 tablespoons of lightly toasted sesame seeds

Juice of 2 lime

1 cup of sliced green onion

2 ripe Hass avocado (cubed)

2 (16-ounce) bag frozen shelled edamame (thawed)

2 teaspoons of grated fresh ginger

½ cup of rice wine vinegar

6 tablespoons of extra virgin olive oil

Pinch of salt and freshly ground black pepper

6 tablespoons of chopped fresh parsley

10 to 16 small radishes (sliced)

Directions

1. First, you bring about 8 cups of water to boil, in a medium saucepan then add the edamame.
2. After which, you boil only for a couple of minutes — you want them cooked through but still firm.
3. After that, you drain the edamame and allow to cool to room temperature.
4. At this point, you whisk together the rice wine vinegar, ginger, oil, garlic, lime, honey, and salt and pepper in a small bowl (for me I prefer using an immersion blender to get the dressing completely emulsified, but a fork or whisk and a strong arm will accomplish the same thing).

5. This is when you set your dressing aside.
6. Furthermore, you add the cooled edamame, parsley, avocado, green onion, radishes, and a sprinkling of sesame seeds.
7. After which you stir them gently together until combined.
8. Then you add the dressing a few large spoonful's at a time, tossing slightly between spoonful's, until you have the desired amount for your salad.
9. Finally, you serve and enjoy!

VEGAN REV' DEIT RECIPES

Avocado and Chickpea Salad Sandwiches
Yields: 8-12 sandwiches, depending on how big you make them

Ingredients

2 large ripe avocado

4 tablespoons of chopped green onion

Salt and pepper (to taste)

Fresh spinach leaves or preferably other sandwich toppings: lettuce, sprouts, tomato slices, etc.

2 (15-ounce) can chickpeas

½ cup of fresh cilantro (chopped)

Juice from 2 limes

Bread of your choice

Directions

1. First, you rinse and drain the chickpeas.
2. After which you add them to a large bowl.
3. After that you pit the avocado and using your knife, score the flesh to make cubes.
4. Then you scoop the cubes out of the skin with a spoon.
5. Furthermore, you use a sturdy fork or a potato masher, smash the chickpeas and avocado together.
6. At this point, you add cilantro, green onion, and lime juice to the mash and stir to thoroughly combine.
7. This is when you season with salt and pepper, to taste.
8. Spread the mixture on bread and top with your favorite sandwich toppings, to make it fun.
9. In addition, you can build a traditional sandwich with tomato, lettuce, cucumber and other goodies in the middle, or better still you can make them open-face with toppings like thinly sliced tomatoes, sprouts,

jalapeños, lime zest, a slice of hard-boiled egg, or anything else you can think of.
11. Enjoy

Vegan Twist on the Classic Tuna Sandwich

Ingredients

6 tablespoons of Ann's Brussels Sprouts Relish

4 stalks celery (chopped)

2 cups of cashew cream

6 cups of water

2 (8-ounce) can garbanzo beans

½ cup of minced red onion

4 teaspoons of ground mustard seed

2 (8 ounces) of raw unsalted cashews

Directions

1. First, you drain and wash garbanzo beans and let them dry.
2. After which, you mash the beans with a fork.
3. After that, you chop the celery stalks.
4. If you want to make the cashew cream, I suggest you soak cashews in 6 cups of water.
5. At this point, you drain and reserve water.
6. Then you puree cashews adding about ½ cup of reserved water to create desired consistency.
7. This is when you mix in cashew cream, celery, mustard, onion and relish.
8. Finally, you garnish with sprouts, lettuce, tomatoes and radishes!

Spinach and Avocado Salad with Garlic Mustard Vinaigrette

Yields: 8 servings

Ingredients

2 teaspoons of fine sea salt

1 teaspoon of mustard (preferably Dijon or honey mustard are both great options)

2 Hass avocado (cubed)

2 garlic clove

2 teaspoons of freshly squeezed lemon juice (more to taste)

4 tablespoons of extra-virgin olive oil

12 cups of loosely packed spinach leaves

Directions

1. First, you use a garlic press, to press the cloves and add them to a small bowl.
2. After which you whisk in the lemon juice, mustard, and a pinch of salt.
3. After that, you continue to whisk until the salt is dissolved, then whisk in the oil until the dressing is emulsified.
4. At this point, you place the spinach leaves in a large bowl and add the dressing, tossing to coat all the leaves.
5. Then you add the cubed avocado and gently toss.
6. Furthermore, you season with a little more salt or lemon juice to taste.
7. Finally, you serve in a bowl or, to add a rustic picnic flare to the meal, use mason jars (NOTE: a mason jar is the perfect way to carry this salad with you to work for lunch)
8. Enjoy!

Mango Avocado Salad

Ingredients

4 avocados (cubed)

¼ cup of Cilantro Lime Dressing

4 mangos (cubed)

½ cup of red cabbage (chopped)

Directions:

1. The first thing you do is to cube your mangos.
2. After which you basically do the same thing to the avocado.
3. However, to consider with the avocados for this recipe: you want them to be just ripe. If they are overly ripe, they will get all mushy when you are tossing the salad.
4. At this point, you add the 4 mangos cubed, 4 avocados cubed, ½ cup chopped red cabbage and half of the dressing.
5. After that, you toss it lightly, adding more dressing if desired.
6. Enjoy!

Avocado and Cucumber Salad with Cilantro-Ginger Dressing

Ingredients

½ cup of cilantro leaves (chopped)

12 cloves garlic (crushed)

4 large cucumbers (chopped in 1/2-inch cubes)

8 celery stalks (thinly sliced on a diagonal)

4 avocados (halved, pitted and sliced)

2 medium tomato, sliced (it is optional)

2 bunch cilantro (leaves left on sprigs)

½ cup of ginger (peeled and chopped)

2 tablespoons of extra-virgin olive oil

2 teaspoons of fine sea salt

4 tablespoons of freshly squeezed lime juice

½ cup of fresh basil leaves (sliced)

Directions

1. First, you combine cilantro sprigs, ginger, olive oil and garlic in a bowl.
2. After which you muddle together until everything is well mashed.
3. After that, you add cucumbers and 2 teaspoons of salt.
4. This is when you stir to mix, cover the bowl and set it aside, stirring occasionally, for about 35 minutes.
5. At this point, you uncover the bowl and discard the cilantro sprigs.
6. Then you mix in celery and lime juice.
7. Furthermore, you season with more salt, if desired.
8. If you want to serve, I suggest you divide the avocado and optional tomato slices on the plates.
9. After that, you spoon the cucumber salad over the slices.

10. Finally, you garnish with the chopped cilantro and basil.
11. Then you serve and enjoy!

Tuscan White Bean Soup
Ingredients

2 small yellow onions (finely chopped)

8 garlic cloves (minced)

2 teaspoons of dried thyme

2 teaspoons of dried ground sage

4 tomatoes (seeded and chopped)

2 can cannellini beans (drained and rinsed)

2 pinches of salt and pepper, to taste

4 tablespoons of extra virgin olive oil

4 stalks celery stalk (diced)

4 teaspoons of dried oregano

2 teaspoons of dried basil

4 carrots (diced)

10 cups of vegetable stock

2 tablespoons of finely chopped sage (for garnish)

Directions

1. First, you heat the olive oil in a large pot over medium-high heat.
2. After which you add the onion, celery, and garlic.
3. After that, you cook these for about 3 minutes or until the onions turn translucent.
4. Then you add the basil, sage, oregano, thyme, carrots and tomatoes and stir to combine.
5. At this point, you cook for about 5 minutes, stirring occasionally.

6. Furthermore, you add the vegetable stock and cannellini beans, and bring the soup to a simmer.
7. After which you simmer for about 10 minutes, stirring occasionally.
8. This is when you place ½ of the soup in a blender and blend until creamy.
9. Then you return it to the pot and stir well to incorporate it.
10. In addition, you taste, and add salt and pepper as necessary.
11. Finally, you ladle the soup into bowls and garnish with a few leaves of fresh sage or basil.

Enjoy!

Savory Bite-Sized Quinoa and Kale Patties

Ingredients

4 cups of water

2/3 cup of Parmesan cheese

6 cloves of garlic (minced)

2 cups of steamed kale, chopped (or preferably Swiss chard or spinach)

2 tablespoons of extra virgin olive oil

2 cups of quinoa

8 eggs (whisked)

6 scallions (thinly sliced)

1 teaspoon of fine sea salt

2 cups of breadcrumbs

Optional toppings: cilantro, avocado, salsa Verde, lemon juice, garlic oil

Directions

1. First, you bring the 4 cups of water and the quinoa to a boil in a medium pot.
2. After which you reduce the heat to low, cover and simmer for about 15 minutes or until the quinoa has absorbed all the water.
3. After that, you allow to cool to room temperature.
4. At this point, you mix together the cooked quinoa, scallions, eggs, cheese, garlic, salt, steamed kale, and breadcrumbs in a large bowl.
5. This is when you let everything sit for a few minutes to absorb the liquid, creating a moist (but not runny) batter.
6. Furthermore, you heat the oil in a large sauté pan over medium-low heat.
7. After which you form the patties using your hands, and place them into the pan.

8. Make sure you leave plenty of room between the patties, and cook them for about 7-8 minutes on one side, or until golden brown.
9. Then you flip them over and repeat on the other side.
10. At this point, when both sides are golden and crisp, then you remove the patties and place them on a wire rack to cool.
11. This you repeat until all the batter is used.
12. Finally, you serve warm or room temperature with salsa, aioli, or other favorite toppings.
13. Enjoy!

Warm Wheat Berry Salad with Mushrooms and White Wine

Ingredients

2 tablespoons of extra-virgin olive oil

2 cups of sliced mushrooms

4 teaspoons of coarsely chopped parsley

2 cups of wheat berries

1 cup of chopped white onions

1 cup of white wine (make sure it is vegan)

Kosher salt and freshly ground black pepper

Directions

1. First, you rinse the wheat berries by placing them in a strainer and running them under cold water.
2. After which in a bring 2.5 quarts of water to a boil in a large soup pot.
3. After that, you add the wheat berries and simmer for about 50 minutes or until softened to al dente texture.
4. At this point, you drain them and set aside in a bowl to cool to room temperature.
5. This is when you heat the olive oil in a medium skillet over low heat.
6. Then you add the onions and cook, stirring frequently, for about 3 minutes or until they are translucent.
7. Furthermore, you stir in the mushrooms and cook for about 1-2 minutes or until they begin to sweat.
8. After that, you add the white wine and simmer for 10 minutes until the wine is mostly absorbed.
9. In addition, you add the onions and mushrooms to the wheat berries in a large bowl.
10. Then you add the chopped parsley, and a pinch of salt and pepper and serve warm.

Note: This salad will keep in the fridge for up to 1 week, and can make an excellent leftover for cold lunches during the week.

Lentil Salad with Lemon-Rosemary Vinaigrette

For the vinaigrette

2 tablespoons of fresh minced rosemary
1 cup of extra virgin olive oil

Juice of 4 lemons (about ½ cup)
Fine sea salt

For the lentils

4 shallots (cut lengthwise into thin wedges)
Fine sea salt and freshly ground black pepper

6 cups of coarsely chopped carrots

4 tablespoons of extra virgin olive oil

3 cups of small brown lentils (or better still French green Puy lentils)

2 bay leaves

2 clove garlic (crushed flat but left whole)

Directions:

Directions on how to make the vinaigrette:

1. First, you whisk together the lemon juice, rosemary, and 2 teaspoons salt in a bowl.
2. After which you slowly drizzle in the olive oil, whisking constantly until emulsified.
3. After that, you let stand at room temperature while you make the salad.
4. Meanwhile, you heat the oven to a temperature of 425F.
5. Then you add the carrots and shallots to a baking dish and drizzle with the olive oil, and toss to coat.
6. At this point, you season with 1 teaspoon of salt and a grinding of pepper.
7. Furthermore, you spread out into a single layer and roast until browned in spots and tender but not mushy, about 20 minutes.

8. After which you remove from the oven and tent loosely with aluminum foil to keep warm.
9. In the meantime, you combine the lentils, garlic, bay leaf, and 8 cups of water in a saucepan, and bring to a boil over a medium-high heat.
10. In addition, you reduce the heat to medium-low, cover, and cook at a gentle simmer for about 12-15 minutes until the lentils are almost tender, but still slightly undercooked.
11. After that, you stir in 1 ½ teaspoon salt, recover and cook for about 10 minutes longer until the lentils are tender but still hold their shape.
12. This is when you drain the lentils in a colander placed in the sink.
13. Then you discard the bay leaf and the garlic and then transfer lentils to a large salad bowl and add the carrots and shallots.
14. Finally, you pour the vinaigrette over the salad and toss gently to combine.
15. Make sure you serve warm.

Mushroom soup with White Beans

Ingredients:

2 tablespoons of olive oil

2 small onion (finely chopped)

2 tablespoons of flour

2 cups of white beans

Salt and Pepper to taste

1 ¼ lb. of mushrooms (about 8 cups)

2 tablespoons of butter

2 - 4 cloves garlic (minced)

8 cups of vegetable stock

1 cup of half and half (or preferably whipping cream)

Directions:

1. First, you clean the mushrooms and slice half of them.
2. After which you finely chop the other half.
3. After that, heat the olive oil in a large saucepan set over medium-high heat and add the butter.
4. Then when the foam subsides, you add the onion, garlic, and both sliced and chopped mushrooms.
5. Furthermore, you reduce the heat slightly and sauté until the moisture evaporates and the mushrooms begin to turn golden.
6. Then you add the flour and cook, stirring to coat the mushrooms, for another minute.
7. In addition, you add the stock and beans and bring to a simmer.
8. At this point, you reduce the heat to low and cook for about 15 minutes.
9. Finally, you turn off the heat and stir in the cream.

10. After which you season with salt and pepper and serve immediately.
11. Enjoy!

Roasted Brussels sprouts with Orange Butter Sauce

Ingredients

4 tablespoons of olive oil

4 teaspoons of balsamic vinegar

2 tablespoons of fresh-squeezed orange juice (I prefer a Cara orange; try a variety on the sweet side!)

4 tablespoons of unsalted butter cut into small cubes (feel free to try a vegan version of this recipe using olive-oil based "butter" such as Smart Balance. Remember that it won't be as creamy but it will carry the orange flavor throughout the Brussels.)

2 lb. of small Brussels sprouts (trimmed and halved lengthwise)

1 teaspoon of salt

2 tablespoon of pure maple syrup

1 teaspoon of grated orange zest

Directions

1. Meanwhile, you heat oven to a temperature of 475 degrees Fahrenheit.
2. After which you line a large baking sheet with parchment paper.
3. After that, you toss the Brussels sprouts in a large bowl with the olive oil and salt until coated.
4. At this point, you line them on the baking sheet, cut-side down, in a single layer.
5. Then you roast them for about 15 minutes, until tender when poked with a fork and the outer leaves are crispy brown.
6. This is when you put them in a mixing bowl.
7. Furthermore, you combine in a small saucepan the balsamic vinegar, orange juice, syrup, and zest.
8. After which you heat over medium-low heat until you see steam rise and it is hot, but not yet simmering.

9. Then you remove from heat and whisk in the butter, adding a few cubes at a time and allowing them to melt as you whisk before adding more.
10. In addition, once all the butter is added, the sauce will be thick and creamy, and a dark brown.
11. This is when you pour the sauce over the Brussels in the mixing bowl and gently stir until the sprouts soak up the sauce.
12. Finally, you serve, and enjoy!

Chickpeas Simmered in Masala Sauce

Ingredients

1 ¼ teaspoons of whole cumin seeds

2 teaspoons of finely grated fresh ginger

2/3 teaspoon of cayenne pepper

2 cups of finely chopped tomatoes

2 teaspoons of fine sea salt

2 teaspoons of lemon juice

6 tablespoons of extra virgin olive oil

2 cups of finely chopped onions

1 ¼ teaspoons of ground coriander

½ teaspoons of ground turmeric

2 cups of water

5 cups of cooked, drained chickpeas

1 teaspoon of garam masala

Directions

1. First, you heat the olive oil, in a frying pan over medium heat then add in the cumin seeds.
2. After which you give them a stir and let them toast for about 10 seconds.
3. After that, you add in the onions, stir them and fry until they begin to turn brown at the edges.
4. This is when you add the ginger, cayenne, coriander, and turmeric and give the spices a quick stir to combine them all with the onion.

5. At this point, you add in the tomatoes, water and salt.
6. Then you stir to combine everything and bring the mixture to a boil.
7. Furthermore, you cover the pan, turn the heat to low, and let the mixture simmer for about 10 minutes.
8. After that, you add in the chickpeas and bring the mixture back up to a boil.
9. Then you turn the heat back down to low, cover and let simmer for about 15 minutes.
10. Finally, you add the garam masala and lemon juice, stir it in, and let it all cook uncovered for another 5 minutes or so.

NOTE: You can enjoy this dish on its own or better still you can serve it over a bed of steamed rice.

Braised Coconut Spinach with Chickpeas and Lemon

Ingredients

2 small yellow onions (finely chopped)

2 tablespoons of freshly grated ginger

2 large lemons, zested and juiced (about 4 tablespoons juice)

2 (14-oz) can chickpeas (drained)

2 (14-oz) can coconut milk

    2 teaspoons of ground ginger

4 teaspoons of olive oil

8 cloves garlic (peeled and minced)

1 cup of sun-dried tomatoes (chopped)

2 dried hot red pepper (or preferably dash of red pepper flakes, optional)

2 pounds of baby spinach

    2 teaspoons of salt (or to taste)

Directions

1. First, you heat the olive oil in a Dutch oven or heavy pot on medium-high heat.
2. After which you add the onion and cook until it is translucent and just beginning to brown.
3. After that, you add the garlic, sun-dried tomatoes, ginger, lemon zest and red pepper.
4. Then you cook the mixture for about 3 minutes, stirring frequently.

5. At this point, you toss in the chickpeas and turn the heat up to high, cooking until the chickpeas turn golden and are thoroughly coated with the onion and spice mixture.
6. This is when you add in the spinach a handful at a time, waiting for it to wilt a little before adding the next handful.
7. Furthermore, you stir it in to incorporate it into the mix.
8. After which you pour in the coconut milk, ground ginger, salt, and lemon juice.
9. Then you bring the pot to a simmer, then turn the heat to medium low and let it simmer for about 10 minutes.
10. Finally, you give it a taste and adjust the lemon juice, salt or other spices as needed.
11. Make sure you serve the dish on its own or ladle it over a bed of rice.
12. Enjoy!

Fingerling Potato Salad with Green Chili-Cilantro Salsa

Ingredients:
8 tablespoons of cider vinegar
4 cups of fresh cilantro sprigs (coarsely chopped)
½ cup of extra-virgin olive oil

8 lb. of fingerling potatoes (or preferably other small boiling potatoes)

6 fresh jalapeño chills (with seeds and ribs removed from 4 of them)

3 shallots (coarsely chopped)

2 garlic clove (coarsely chopped)

Directions:
1. First, you cover potatoes with salted cold water by 1 inch, then simmer for about 10 to 15 minutes until just tender,
2. After which you drain potatoes and rinse under cold water until slightly cooled.
3. After that, you halve lengthwise and while still warm gently toss with 2 tablespoons of vinegar.
4. At this point, you cool potatoes to room temperature, then season with salt and pepper.
5. Then while potatoes cook, you coarsely chop jalapeños and pulse in a food processor with cilantro, shallots, garlic, oil, and remaining 6 tablespoons vinegar until finely chopped.
6. Finally, you toss potatoes with salsa and enjoy!

VEGAN REV' DEIT RECIPES

Five-minute vegan pancake

Ingredients

1 cups of sugar

1 teaspoon of baking soda

6 tablespoons of vegetable oil

1 cups of water

1 ½ cups of flour

3 tablespoons of cocoa

½ teaspoon of salt

1 teaspoons of vanilla

1 tablespoons of vinegar

Directions

1. First, you sift dry ingredients into an ungreased (8x8) pan.
2. After which you make 3 holes in dry ingredients.
3. In the first hole, you put 6 teaspoons of oil.
4. In the second hole, you put 1 teaspoon of vanilla.
5. In the third hole, you put 1 Tablespoon of vinegar.
6. After that, you pour 1 cup of water over all and stir until smooth.
7. Then you bake at a temperature of 350 degrees for 35 minutes.
8. Finally, you frost or sprinkle with confectioner's sugar.
9. Can double recipe if you wish.

Baja Black Beans, Corn and Rice

Ingredients

2 (15 ounce) can black beans, (rinsed and drained)

8 fresh tomatoes (diced)

1 cup cilantro (chopped)

4 tablespoons of fresh lime juice

1 teaspoon salt

4 dashes of hot sauce

12 cups of cooked brown rice

2 (15 ounce) can corn, drained

1 cup of red onion (chopped)

2 jalapeno pepper (seeded and diced)

2 tablespoons of olive oil

½ teaspoon of fresh ground pepper

Directions

1. First, you cook brown rice.
2. After which you combine in a medium bowl the tomatoes, onion, black beans, corn, cilantro, jalapeno, lime juice, oil, salt, pepper and hot sauce.
3. If you want to serve, I suggest you place a scoop of hot rice in a bowl or on a plate, top with a generous scoop of the black bean mixture.
4. Then you stir together before eating.

Roasted Cauliflower & 16 Roasted Cloves of Garlic

Ingredients

16 garlic cloves (peeled and lightly crushed)

1 teaspoon of salt

More olive oil, to drizzle if you wish

1 large cauliflower (it should be trimmed and cut into bite size pieces, washed with water still on)

1-2 teaspoons of minced fresh rosemary

¼-½ teaspoon of black pepper

¼ cup olive oil, (adding more to taste)

Directions

1. First, you mix oil, rosemary, salt, pepper and garlic together.
2. After which you toss in cauliflower and place in a large casserole dish in one layer.
3. After that, you roast in a preheated oven at a temperature of 450 degrees for 20 minutes.
4. Then you give a toss and bake for about 10 more minutes.

Roasted Green Beans

Ingredients

1 -2 tablespoons of olive oil (or preferably just enough to lightly coat beans)

½ teaspoon of fresh ground pepper (or preferably to taste, omit if using Mrs. Dash)

2 lbs. of green beans

1 teaspoon of kosher salt (or preferably to taste, may substitute with Mrs. Dash if desired)

Directions

1. Meanwhile, you heat oven to a temperature of 400°F.
2. After which you wash, dry well, and trim green beans.
3. After that, you put green beans on a jelly roll pan.
4. Then you drizzle with olive oil and sprinkle with salt and pepper to taste (I prefer them salty so I use about 1 1/2 teaspoons of salt and about 8-10 grinds of the pepper mill).

Note: Mrs. Dash may be a good substituted for salt and pepper as desired.

5. At this point, you use your hands to be sure all the beans are evenly coated and spread them out into 1 layer.
6. Furthermore, you roast for about 20-25 minutes, turning after 15 minutes, until beans are fairly brown in spots and somewhat shriveled.
7. Finally, you serve hot or at room temperature.

Good Vegetarian Meatloaf (Really!)

Ingredients

1 teaspoons of salt

1 small onion (diced)

¾ cup grated cheddar cheese (or preferably ¾ cup Swiss cheese, cheese or ¾ cup Monterey jack cheese or ¾ cup American cheese)

4 ½ ounces of spaghetti sauce (or preferably 4 ½ ounces' tomato sauce)

1 teaspoon of dried basil

¼ teaspoon of black pepper

2 cups of water

1 cup of lentils

1 cup quick-cooking oat

1 egg (beaten)

1 teaspoon of garlic powder

1 tablespoon of dried parsley

½ teaspoon of seasoning salt

Directions

1. First, you add salt to water and boil in a saucepan.
2. After which you add lentils and simmer covered for 25-30 minutes, until lentils are soft and most of water is evaporated.
3. After that you remove from fire and drain, then you partially mash lentils.
4. At this point, you scrape into mixing bowl and allow to cool slightly.

5. Then you stir in onion, oats and cheese until mixed.
6. This is when you add egg, basil, tomato sauce, garlic, parsley, seasoning salt and pepper and mix well.
7. Furthermore, you spoon into loaf pan that has been generously sprayed with Pam (non-stick cooking spray) or well-greased.
8. After that, you smooth top with back of spoon and bake at 350 degrees for 30- 45 minutes until top of loaf is dry, firm and golden brown.
9. Then you cool in pan on rack for about 10 minutes.
10. Finally, you run a sharp knife around edges of pan then turn out loaf onto serving platter.

Sweet Cornbread

Ingredients

1 ¼ cup of sugar

2 tablespoons of baking powder

2 ½ cups of milk

6 tablespoons of butter (or preferably 6 tablespoons of margarine, melted)

3 cups of flour

1 cup of cornmeal

1 teaspoon of salt

4 large eggs (lightly beaten)

2/3 cup of oil

Directions

1. Meanwhile, you heat oven to a temperature of 350°F.
2. After which you grease 8-inch square baking pan.
3. After that, you combine flour, baking powder, sugar, corn meal and salt in medium bowl.
4. At this point, you combine milk, eggs, oil and butter in small bowl and mix well.
5. Then you add to flour mixture and stir just until blended.
6. Furthermore, you pour into baking pan.
7. After that, you bake for about 35 minutes or until wooden pick comes out clean.

NOTE: As for corn muffins, I suggest you spoon batter into muffin cups 2/3 full.

8. Then you bake for about 18-20 minutes or until wooden pick comes out clean.

9. Finally, you cool for about 5 minutes before removing from pans.

Vegetarian Lasagna
Ingredients

½ cup of grated carrot

6 cooked lasagna noodles

1 (16 ounce) package frozen chopped spinach (thawed and well drained)

1 ½ cups of thinly sliced zucchini

½ cup of grated parmesan cheese

1 ½ quarts spaghetti sauce (or better still your favorite homemade or jar spaghetti sauce)

½ teaspoon of oregano

1 (16 ounce) container ricotta cheese

2 eggs

1 cups of sliced fresh mushrooms

3 cups of shredded part-skim mozzarella cheese

Directions

1. First, you mix carrots, oregano, and spaghetti sauce together.
2. After that, you mix Ricotta, spinach, and eggs together in separate bowl.
3. Then you spread ½ cup spaghetti sauce in bottom of 9 x 13-inch baking dish.
4. After which you layer 3 lasagna noodles, ½ remaining sauce, ½ sliced zucchini, ½ Ricotta mixture, ½ Mozzarella, ½ sliced mushrooms, and ½ Parmesan.
5. At this point, you repeat layers with remaining ingredients.

6. Bake in a temperature of 350 degrees' oven for about 45 minutes.

Vegetarian Chili
Ingredients

1 medium onion (chopped)

1 cups of chopped sweet red pepper

3 tablespoons of olive oil

1 (about 15 ounce) can of tomato sauce

1 (about 15 ounce) can of black beans, drained

¼ cup of fresh cilantro (minced)

3 tablespoons of chili powder

1 teaspoon of cumin

2 medium zucchini (chopped)

1 cup green pepper (chopped)

3 cloves garlic, (minced)

2 (about 28 ounce) cans of Italian stewed tomatoes, cut up

1 (about 15 ounce) can pinto beans (drained)

1 jalapeno pepper (seeded and chopped)

¼ cup of fresh parsley (minced)

1 tablespoon of sugar

1 teaspoon of salt

Directions

1. First, in lg pot, you sauté zucchini, onion, peppers and garlic in oil until tender.
2. After which you stir in all remaining ingredients.
3. After that, you bring to a boil.
4. Then you reduce heat, cover and simmer for about 30 minutes, stirring occasionally.

Vegetarian Tacos
Ingredients

2 small yellow onion (chopped)

2 red peppers (or preferably 2 green pepper, chopped)

2 garlic clove (minced)

6 -10 tablespoons of your favorite chunky salsa

1 teaspoon chili powder (I prefer the color this gives the beans)

16 taco shells

2 tablespoons of olive oil

2 stalk celery (chopped)

2 jalapeno pepper, de-seeded, minced (or preferably to taste-can substitute hot sauce or a dash of cayenne for the heat)

2 (19 ounce) can of garbanzo beans (drained)

1 teaspoon of cumin

1 teaspoon of ground coriander (preferably your choice)

Ingredients for Taco Toppings

Shredded iceberg lettuce

Hot sauce

Tomatoes

Sour cream

Shredded cheddar cheese

Salsa

Fresh cilantro (chopped)

Black olives

Directions

1. First, you heat oil in a large fry pan, over medium heat.
2. After which you cook the red or green pepper, onion, celery, jalapeno, and garlic until softened.
3. After that, you add garbanzo beans, spices, and a couple teaspoon of salsa.
4. Then you stir until heated through.

NOTE: I prefer fitting the taco shells in a baking pan, spoon in filling evenly into the shells and bake in a 300°F oven for about 5 minutes or so.

5. By so doing it helps the shells from falling apart when you take the first bite.
6. Finally, you remove from oven and top with your favorite toppings.

Vegetarian "meatballs"

Ingredients

1 (about 1 ¼ ounce) of envelope Lipton Onion Soup Mix

¾ cup of chopped walnuts

2 (about 1 ¼ ounce) of envelopes vegetarian broth (I prefer Washington brown broth)

4 eggs (slightly beaten)

2 cups of grated cheddar cheese

1 cup of dry Italian style breadcrumbs

Directions

1. First, you mix the 4 eggs, Lipton Onion Soup Mix, cheddar cheese, walnuts and dry Italian style breadcrumbs together in order.
2. After which you refrigerate for about 30 minutes.
3. After that, you form into 1-1/4 inch balls and place on baking sheet sprayed with Pam.
4. Then you bake in 400-degree oven for about 20 minutes until brown.
5. (At least it May be frozen now.)
6. At this point, you place meatballs in casserole and cover with 2-3 cups boiling water and 2-3 cubes or envelopes vegetarian brown broth.
7. Remember the meatballs should be within 1/2 inch of being covered with liquid.
8. Bake, covered, at a temperature of 350 degrees for 1 hour (or about 1-1/2 hrs. if meatballs are frozen).
9. Or in the other way round, meatballs may be prepared in a crockpot on high setting for 1 hour (or better still 1-1/2 if frozen).

Vegetarian Split Pea Soup

Ingredients

14 cups of water (or 14 cups vegetable stock)

4 teaspoons of salt

4 cups of onions (minced)

6 stalks celery (minced)

2 potatoes (diced)

2-8 tablespoons of balsamic vinegar, to taste (or preferably red wine vinegar)

6 cups of dried split peas

2 bay leaf

2 teaspoons of dry mustard

8 medium garlic cloves (minced)

4 medium carrots (sliced)

Fresh ground black pepper

Optional toppings

Fresh ripe tomatoes, diced (it is optional)

Fresh parsley, minced (it is optional)

Sesame oil (it is optional)

Directions

1. First, you place the dried split peas, water or vegetable stock, bay leaf, salt and mustard in a large pot.

2. After which you bring to a boil, reduce heat to low, and simmer, partially covered for about 20 minutes, stirring occasionally to prevent split peas from sticking to bottom of pot.
3. After that, you add onions, carrots, garlic, celery, and potato. (NOTE: You can sauté these first or better still add them in directly if you want a fat free soup).
4. At this point, you partially cover and allow to simmer for about 40 minutes, stirring occasionally (NOTE: You may need to add extra water).
5. Then you season to taste with pepper and vinegar.
6. Finally, you serve with a drizzle of sesame oil, diced tomato and minced parsley.

VEGAN REV' DEIT RECIPES

Vegetarian Taco Soup
Ingredients

2 (30 ounce) can navy beans

2 small onion (chopped)

2 (2 ½ ounce) package taco seasoning mix

2 (30 ounce) can black- eyed peas or 2 (30 ounce) can purple hull peas

2 (28 ounce) can tomato sauce

2 (2 ounce) package ranch dressing mix

2 (30 ounce) can black beans

2 (30 ounce) can green beans

2 (20 ounce) can Rotel Tomatoes

2 (30 ounce) can pinto beans

2 (30 ounce) can corn

4 cups water

Suggested condiments of your choice

Grated cheese

Sliced jalapeno

Crushed tortilla chips (or better still Fritos corn chips)

Sour cream

Picante sauce (or Tabasco sauce)

Green onion

Directions

1. First, you drain and rinse the black beans, navy beans, green beans, onion and Rotel tomatoes and taco seasoning mix in a large colander.
2. After which you put in a crockpot or large pot.
3. After that, you add all other ingredients, stirring to mix well.
4. Then you simmer about 30 minutes to an hour or cook in your crockpot on high for 2 hours.

Best Vegetarian Pot Stickers

Ingredients

2 tablespoons of minced ginger

2 cups of white cabbage, (shredded)

2 cups of chopped garlic sprout (or preferably 2 cups chives)

2 teaspoons of sesame oil

2 package of wonton skins (also called gyoza)

Canola oil

2 red onions, (sliced)

2 cups of sliced shiitake mushroom

2 cups of carrot, (shredded)

2 teaspoons white pepper

½ cup of chopped cilantro

Salt

Directions

1. First, you add a little oil in a wok or large sauté pan, and sauté onions and ginger.
2. After which you add the mushrooms and stir.
3. After that, you add the cabbage, carrots and chives, season.
4. At this point, when mixture is soft, you place in colander to drain.
5. Then you add the sesame oil and cilantro when mixture is cooled.
6. Check for seasoning.

VEGAN REV' DEIT RECIPES

7. If you want to use the gyoza skins, I suggest you make half-moon dumplings keeping the bottom flat.
8. After that, you coat with oil and place dumplings in a hot non-stick pan.
9. Then when bottom gets brown, you add ½ cup of water and immediately cover (Note: this will steam the dumplings).
10. You should carefully watch the dumplings and completely evaporate the water so that the bottom gets crispy again and sticks to the pot.
11. Finally, you serve hot with soy sauce and vinegar for dipping.

Uncle Bill's Vegetarian Minestrone Soup

Ingredients:

1 ½ cups of chopped onion

4 cups of diced zucchini

2 cups of canned cannellini beans (or 2 cups you may use other white beans)

2 teaspoons of dried basil (or preferably 4 tablespoons of finely chopped fresh basil)

½ teaspoon of salt

56 fluid ounces canned plum tomatoes (dice and include liquid)

½ cup of uncooked ditalini (or preferably ½ cup of elbow macaroni)

2 tablespoons of extra virgin olive oil

6 cups of water

2 cups of diced carrot (peeled)

1 ¼ cup of diced celery

½ teaspoon of dried oregano

¼ teaspoon of fresh coarse ground black pepper

4 garlic cloves, (minced)

Directions

1. First, you heat oil in a large saucepan over medium-high heat.

2. After which you add chopped onion and sauté for 4 minutes or until just lightly browned.
3. After that, you add water, canellini beans, zucchini, carrots, celery, basil, oregano salt, pepper, tomatoes and garlic.
4. This is when you bring to boil; reduce heat, cover and simmer on medium-low heat for 25 minutes, stirring occasionally.
5. At this point, you add macaroni, cover and cook an additional 10 minutes.
6. Then you adjust spices to suit your taste.
7. Make sure you serve hot.

Vegetarian BLT
Ingredients

6 -8 slices tomatoes

2 -4 tablespoons of mayonnaise

Black pepper (if desired)

4 slices of white bread (toasted)

2 -4 lettuce leaf

2 -4 slice of provolone cheese

Directions

1. First, you spray a non-stick skillet with plenty of non-stick spray.
2. After which you place the cheese in a single layer in the center.
3. After that, you heat the skillet over medium heat.
4. At this point, when the cheese bubbles and is crunchy and hard on the bottom, you flip to the other side.
5. Remember do not try flipping the cheese before the bottom is totally solid or you will wind up with a goopy mess.
6. Then once both sides of the cheese are crunchy, I suggest you assemble the sandwich with the lettuce, tomato, and "bacon" (cheese), and the mayo spread over the bread.
7. Enjoy

Vegetarian Paella

Ingredients

2 medium eggplant, (cut into large chunks)

2 onion (chopped)

2 yellow pepper (finely chopped)

450g Arborio rice

2 (38 ounce) can diced tomatoes

2 cups mushroom, (sliced)

2 (38 ounce) can chickpeas, (rinsed and drained)

2 pinches saffron

6 tablespoons of authentico olive oil (or better still your favorite kind)

4 garlic cloves (crushed)

2 red bell pepper, (finely chopped)

4 teaspoons paprika

5 cups of vegetable broth

Salt and pepper

2 cups of green beans, (cut into segments)

Directions

1. First, you pour 6 tablespoons water over saffron in a small bowl and set aside.
2. After which you sprinkle salt over the eggplant chunks and let stand in a colander for about 30 minutes.

3. After that, you rinse and drain.
4. At this point, you heat the oil in a large frying pan and sauté the onion, garlic, peppers and eggplant for about 5 minutes.
5. Then you sprinkle with paprika and toss.
6. Furthermore, you add the rice, then incorporate the tomatoes, vegetable stock, saffron and season with salt and pepper to taste.
7. After which you bring to a boil and simmer for about 15 minutes, uncovered, stirring frequently.
8. In addition, you fold in the mushrooms, green beans and chickpeas.
9. Finally, you cook for another 15 minutes and serve immediately.

Southwest Vegetarian Bake

Ingredients

3 cups of water

2 (22 ounce) can mexicorn, drained

2 cups of salsa

2 cups of cheddar cheese (shredded)

1 cup red onion, (chopped)

2 cups of Mexican blend cheese (shredded)

1 ½ cup of brown rice (uncooked)

2 (30 ounce) can black beans (rinsed and drained)

2 (20 ounce) can diced tomatoes with green chilies

2 cups sour cream

½ teaspoon of pepper

2 (4 ½ ounce) can black olives (sliced, drained)

Directions

1. First, you bring rice and water to a boil in a large saucepan.
2. After which you reduce heat; cover and simmer for about 35-40 minutes, until tender.
3. After that, you combine beans, sour cream, corn, tomatoes, salsa, cheddar, pepper and rice in a bowl.
4. Then you transfer to a 5-quart baking dish coated with nonstick spray.
5. This is when you sprinkle onions and olives over top.
6. Bake, uncovered, at a temperature of 350°F for 30 minutes.
7. Finally, you sprinkle Mexican cheese over top.
8. Bake for about 5-10 minutes longer, until cheese is melted.

9. After which you let stand 10 minutes.

Vegetarian Black Bean Soup

Ingredients

2 tablespoons of olive oil

2 cups of chopped onions

2 cups of chopped celery

2 cups of diced carrots

3 bay leaves

½ teaspoon of salt

⅛ teaspoon of cumin

1 teaspoon dried cilantro

2 cups of dried black beans

5 garlic cloves (minced)

2 cups of chopped red bell peppers

¼ cup of chopped celery leaves

10 cups of water

14 ½ ounces of diced tomatoes

½ teaspoon of pepper

1 teaspoon of dried oregano

Directions

1. First, you soak beans overnight; drain.
2. After which you heat oil in a large soup pot.
3. After that, you add in garlic, celery, onion, red peppers, celery leaves and carrots.
4. Then you cover and cook for about 10 minutes, until veggies start to soften.
5. At this point, you add water, salt, pepper, bay leaves, canned tomatoes, cumin, oregano and cilantro.

6. This is when you bring to a boil.
7. Furthermore, you add drained black beans.
8. After that, you bring to a boil and then reduce heat and simmer for about 2 hours or until beans are tender.
9. Finally, you discard bay leaves and serve.

Garbanzo Vegetarian Burgers

Ingredients

2 cups of shredded carrot

4 tablespoons of Italian salad dressing

2 dashes red pepper flakes (it is optional)

2 (16 ounce) can garbanzo beans, (drained)

2/3 cup of seasoned bread crumbs

2 eggs

4 tablespoons of olive oil

Directions

1. First, you mesh garbanzo beans with potato masher or by hand.
2. After which you leave some as slightly large pieces.
3. After that, you stir in carrots, bread crumbs, egg and salad dressing.
4. Then you heat oil in nonstick skillet.
5. Furthermore, you shape into 3-4 patties and brown on both sides.
6. After which, about 3 minutes on each side until browned.
7. Finally, you garnish toasted buns and enjoy a new type burger.

Creamy Tortilla Soup-Vegetarian

Ingredients

2 (14 ½ ounce) cans vegetable broth

1 (16 ounce) can black beans, (drained)

2 teaspoons fresh cilantro (chopped)

Shredded monetary jack cheese

2 (14 1/2 ounce) cans Rotel tomatoes and chilies

1 (16 ounce) can vegetarian refried beans

½ cup of corn (fresh, frozen or canned)

Corn tortilla strips or chips

Directions

1. First, you combine tomatoes, broth, beans and corn in medium saucepan.
2. After which you stir together and bring to a boil.
3. After that, you reduce and bring to a simmer till heated through.
4. Then you turn off heat and stir in the cilantro.
5. Finally, you top each bowl of soup with cheese and crushed tortilla chips. (I prefer up the crushed chips from the bottom of the bag.).

Vegetarian Apple Stir-Fry

Ingredients

2 cups of sliced carrot

2/3 cup of dry roasted salted peanut

2 tablespoons of basil

Soy sauce (it is optional)

4 granny smith apples, (cored and diced)

2 cups of snow peas

4 tablespoons of canola oil

4 cups of cooked brown rice (steamed)

Directions

1. First, you start steaming your brown rice ahead of time.
2. After which you heat canola oil in frying pan on medium heat.
3. After that, you add carrots peanuts and basil stirring frequently for about 5 minutes.
4. Then you add snow peas and cook for another 5 minutes stirring frequently.
5. At this point, you add apples and stir, after which you top rice with mixture.
6. Finally, you add soy sauce if you wish.

Vegetarian Taco Salad - Low Fat

Ingredients

8 ¾ ounces' corn (drained)

2 -3 roma tomatoes (diced)

1 tablespoon of taco seasoning

5 ounces baked corn tortilla chips (or preferably 5 ounces' polenta corn chips, broken)

16 ounces' kidney beans (rinsed and drained)

4 ounces' green chilies

3 green onions (sliced)

⅓ cup of light sour cream

4 -5 cups of mixed greens (shredded)

Directions

1. First, you stir kidney beans, corn, green chilies, tomatoes, green onion, taco seasoning and sour cream (through sour cream) together in a large bowl until combined.
2. After which you gently stir in mixed greens (NOTE: greens will wilt if there are leftovers, so I usually just throw the greens on the serving plate!).
3. After that, you layer chips on serving plates and top with taco mixture.
4. Then you serve with your favorite taco toppings if desired, olives, shredded cheese, taco sauce, etc.

VEGAN REV' DEIT RECIPES

Very Quick Butter Chickpeas (Vegetarian Butter Chicken!)

Ingredients

4 tablespoons of canola oil

4 teaspoons of curry powder

2 teaspoons of ground ginger

600 g condensed tomato soup

600 g chickpeas

1 teaspoon of salt

2 medium onion

2 teaspoons minced garlic

4 teaspoons of garam masala

2 teaspoons ground cumin

1 cup of cream

400g boiled baby potatoes, (cubed)

2-4 tablespoons of chopped coriander

Directions

1. First, you chop the onion very finely while the oil heats in a large pan.
2. After which you add the onion and garlic and cook, stirring frequently, until the onion is starting to brown.
3. After that, you stir in the curry powder and gram masala, ginger and cumin.
4. Then you continue to cook, stirring frequently, for one to two minutes longer.
5. At this point, you tip in the soup, cream, drained chickpeas and potatoes, and leave the sauce to simmer for about five minutes.

6. This is when you add the chopped coriander and salt to taste.
7. Then you serve over steamed basmati rice.
8. Enjoy!

Fabulous Vegetarian Chili

Ingredients

2 medium onion, (chopped)

2 medium carrot (diced)

12 garlic cloves (finely chopped)

2 (31 ounce) can red kidney beans, (undrained)

2 lb. firm tofu (rinsed, patted dry and crumbled)

4 cups of frozen whole kernel corn

2 -4 tablespoons of chili powder

Fresh ground black pepper

4 tablespoons of oil

2 medium green bell pepper, (seeded and chopped)

4 cups of unpeeled unseeded (fresh tomatoes)

2 (16 ounces each) can pinto beans (undrained)

2 (15 ounces each) can crushed tomatoes

4 cups of water (or preferably can use vegetable broth)

4 teaspoons salt (I prefer seasoned salt)

2 tablespoons cumin

½ teaspoon of cayenne pepper

Directions

1. First, you heat oil in a 5-qt Dutch oven.
2. After which you add onions, green peppers and carrots.

3. After that, you sauté over med heat until tender.
4. This is when you add beans, fresh tomatoes, garlic, crushed tomatoes, corn, salt, tofu, water, chili powder, cumin and cayenne pepper.
5. At this point, you simmer for about 45-60 minutes or until done, stirring often, adjusting all seasonings to suit taste.
6. Then about halfway through cooking time you season with black pepper and more salt if needed.

Oven Fried Eggplant (Aubergine)

Ingredients

1 cup of fat-free mayonnaise

2 tablespoons of minced onion

2/3 cup of grated parmesan cheese

2/3 cup of fine dry breadcrumb

1 teaspoon of dried Italian seasoning

Vegetable oil cooking spray

2 lb. of unpeeled eggplant, (sliced-about 24 (1/2 inch slices))

Directions

1. First, you combine the breadcrumb, fat-free mayonnaise and stir well.
2. After which you spread evenly over both sides of eggplant slices.
3. After that, you combine breadcrumbs, cheese, and Italian seasoning in a shallow bowl.
4. Then you dredge eggplant in breadcrumbs mixture.
5. At this point, you place eggplant on a baking sheet coated with cooking spray.
6. Bake at a temperature of 425 degrees for about 12 minutes.
7. Finally, you turn eggplant over; and bake an additional 12 minutes or until golden.

Roasted Brussels sprouts

Ingredients

6 tablespoons of olive oil

1 teaspoon of lemon-pepper seasoning (or better still 1 teaspoon ground black pepper)

3 lbs. of Brussels sprouts.

1- 1 ½ teaspoon of kosher salt

Directions

1. Meanwhile, you heat oven to a temperature of 400°F.
2. After which you cut off the ends of the Brussels sprouts and pull off any yellow outer leaves.
3. After that, you mix them in a bowl with the olive oil, salt, and lemon-pepper seasoning.
4. Then you transfer them to a sheet pan and roast for about 35 to 40 minutes, until crisp outside and tender inside.
5. Make sure you shake the pan from time to time to brown the Brussels sprouts evenly.
6. Finally, you sprinkle with more kosher salt (I prefer these salty like French fries), if you like, and serve hot.

Greek Potatoes (Oven-Roasted and Delicious!)

Ingredients

4 garlic cloves, minced (remember more garlic is a good thing, less garlic is a no-no for this recipe)

1 cup of water

1 lemon (juiced)

Fresh coarse ground black pepper

8 large potatoes peeled, cut into large wedges (about 6-7 wedges per potato)

½ cup of olive oil

1 tablespoon of dried oregano (get the Mediterranean, it's the best!)

Sea salt

Directions

1. Meanwhile, you heat oven to a temperature of 420°F
2. After which you spraying the baking pan with Pam.
3. After that you put all the ingredients into a baking pan large enough to hold them.
4. Then you season generously with sea salt and black pepper.
5. This is when you make sure your hands are very clean and put them in the pan and give everything a toss to distribute.
6. At this point, the garlic will drop into the water/oil solution but its flavor will permeate the potatoes, and this way, it won't burn.
7. Bake for about 40 minutes.
8. Furthermore, when a nice golden-brown crust has formed on the potatoes, you give them a stir to bring the white underside up.
9. After which you season lightly with a bit more sea salt and pepper and just a light sprinkling of oregano.
10. Then you add 1 cup more water if pan appears to be getting dry, and pop back into oven to brown other side of potatoes (this will take about another 40 minutes).

NOTE: Do not be afraid of overcooking the potatoes- they will be delicious.

11. In the other hand, I often melt a bouillon cube in the water; if you do, make sure to cut back some on the salt

Hearty Vegetarian Tofu Chili

Ingredients

2 medium onion (chopped)

2 medium green pepper (chopped)

4 garlic cloves (minced)

2 teaspoons of olive oil

32 ounces extra firm tofu (drained and crumbled)

2 teaspoons of cumin

2 teaspoons of hot sauce

Salt (to taste)

Pepper (to taste)

2 (19 ounces each) can red kidney beans, drained

2 (19 ounces each) can white kidney beans, drained

2 (28 ounces each) can diced tomatoes

2 (14 ounces each) can tomato sauce

6 medium carrots (sliced)

4 tablespoons chili powder

Directions

A. First, you sauté first 4 in medium heat.
B. After which you add tofu, cumin, hot sauce, and salt and pepper.
C. After that, you sauté until crisp and lightly browned (about 10 min).
D. Then you add rest of ingredients (beans, carrots, tomatoes, tomato sauce, and chili powder).
E. Finally, you boil, reduce heat and simmer for about 45 to 55 minutes.

Soy Glazed Tofu and Asparagus

Ingredients

1 teaspoon of cayenne chili pepper flakes

1 ½ cups of extra firm tofu, (cut into 1/2 inch cubes)

2 clove garlic, (minced)

4 tablespoons of soy sauce

4 tablespoons of sesame oil

16 stalks of asparagus, (woody ends snapped off)

2 cups of sliced button mushroom

4 teaspoons of granulated sugar

Directions

1. First, you heat sesame oil and red pepper flakes in nonstick skillet or wok.
2. After which you cut asparagus spears into 1 ½ inch pieces.
3. After that, you add asparagus and tofu to heated sesame oil and stir-fry for about 5 minutes.
4. At this point, you add mushrooms and cook for 3 minutes.
5. This is when you add garlic, sauté, stirring constantly, for about 30 seconds.
6. Furthermore, you mix sugar and soy sauce together in small bowl until combined and add to pan.
7. After which you mix well to coat and stir-fry for about 3-4 minutes.

NOTE: Asparagus should be crisp-tender at this point.

8. Then you serve.

Tofu Egg Salad

Ingredients

1 cup of soy mayonnaise (or preferably regular, your choice)

2 teaspoons of cayenne pepper

4 tablespoons of chopped parsley

Salt and pepper

4 lbs. firm tofu

6 tablespoons Dijon mustard

1 teaspoon of turmeric

2 tablespoons of chopped fresh dill (I've used dried as well)

1 cup green onion, (diced)

Directions

1. Remember, I always drain my tofu first.
2. After which I cut it into ¼ s, wrap it in paper towels on a cookie sheet, with another one on top, weighted down with some heavy canned goods.
3. After that, you let sit in refrigerator for about 10-20 minutes.
4. Then you mash the tofu in a bowl with a wooden spoon.
5. At this point, you mix tofu well with remaining ingredients.
6. Finally, you chill and serve

Marinated Baked Tofu

Ingredients

6-8 tablespoons of soy sauce

2 tablespoons of fresh grated ginger (to taste)

2 tablespoons of rice vinegar

2 tablespoons of olive oil

2 (16 ounces each) package firm tofu (or preferably 2 (16 ounce) package extra firm tofu, in water)

2 -4 minced garlic clove, to taste

2 tablespoons of sesame oil

2 -4 teaspoons of honey (optional) or preferably 2 -4 teaspoons of sugar (it is optional)

Directions

1. First, you drain tofu and cut into 1" cubes.
2. After which you mix all other ingredients together except olive oil.
3. After that you pour marinade over tofu and cover.
4. Then you refrigerate overnight or longer (I left mine for 3 nights).
5. At this point, you lightly grease baking pan or sheet with olive oil.
6. This is when you arrange tofu in single layer on sheet, making sure not to forget the garlic and ginger from the marinade dish.
7. Finally, you bake at a temperature of 350 degrees for 50-60 minutes, flipping tofu at least once during the process, until brown and slightly crispy.

Vegetarian Five Spice Tofu Stir-Fry

Ingredients

4 tablespoons of oyster sauce

2 tablespoons of reduced sodium soy sauce

2 medium tofu (drained)

4 tablespoons of vegetable oil

½ teaspoon of hot pepper flakes

2 (8 ounces) shiitake mushrooms (stemmed and halved)

1 cup of vegetable broth

2 tablespoons of cornstarch

2 teaspoons of brown sugar (packed)

1 teaspoon of five-spice powder

6 garlic cloves, (sliced thinly)

2 head bok choy, chopped (around 2 pounds)

Directions

1. First, you whisk together broth, cornstarch, soy sauce, oyster sauce, sugar and ½ cup water in bowl, set aside.
2. After which you cut tofu into 1-inch cubes, toss with 5 spice powder.
3. After that, you heat half of the oil in wok or skillet over medium high.
4. At this point, you stir-fry tofu for 4 minutes (or until golden).
5. Then you transfer to paper towel lined plate and heat remaining oil over medium high heat.
6. This is when you stir-fry garlic and hot pepper flakes for 30 seconds.
7. Furthermore, you add bok choy and mushrooms, stir-fry for about 3 minutes.
8. Finally, you stir in tofu and broth mixture, bring to boil.
9. After which you reduce heat, cover and simmer until thickened and vegetables are softened (around three minutes).

10. Make sure you serve over rice.

Tibetan Greens with Tofu (Tse Tofu)

Ingredients

4 green onions, (chopped)

4 garlic cloves (chopped)

4 tablespoons soy sauce

½ cup of green peas

½ teaspoon ground black pepper

2 bunch Swiss chard

1 teaspoon paprika

1-inch fresh ginger (chopped)

8 (12 ounce) blocks firm tofu (cut into 1-inch cubes)

2 tablespoons of oil

2 garlic clove, (chopped)

Directions

1. First, you wash the Swiss chard and tear it into pieces, removing the stems.
2. After which you heat a little oil in a frying pan, and stir-fry the green onions, along with the paprika, ginger, and 4 cloves of garlic.
3. After that, you stir in the soy sauce, tofu, and peas.
4. Then in an in a separate frying pan you heat 2 tablespoons of oil until it's very hot.
5. At this point, you stir in the black pepper.
6. Furthermore, you add the Swiss chard, still slightly wet, and toss to coat with the oil and pepper.
7. After which you cover the pan and let it steam for about 30 seconds.
8. Finally, you spread the greens on a serving platter and pour the tofu mixture on top.

Cauliflower with Salsa Verde

Ingredients:

Vegetable oil for frying

½ teaspoon of paprika

6 bushy sprigs of mint

2 cloves garlic (crushed)

2 tablespoons of capers

Salt and pepper (to taste)

1 medium cauliflower

3 tablespoons of gram flour

Generous handful of parsley

Handful of basil

2 tablespoons of Dijon mustard

6 tablespoons of olive oil
2 tablespoons of lemon juice

Directions:

1. First, you break the cauliflower into florets.
2. After which you boil in salted water for a couple of minutes, then drain thoroughly.
3. **If you want to make the sauce:**
4. **First, you** chop the herbs quite finely, but not so small they look like tealeaves, then stir in the garlic, mustard and capers.
5. After which you pour in the olive oil slowly, beating with a fork.

6. After that, you stir in the lemon juice and season with sea salt and black pepper. (**NOTE:** be generous with the seasoning, tasting as you go).
7. Remember that sauce should be bright tasting and piquant.
8. This is when you get the oil hot in a deep pan and toss the cauliflower with the gram flour, a little salt and pepper and the paprika.
9. At this point, when the cauliflower is coated, you fry in the hot oil till crisp, a matter of three or four minutes or so.
10. Finally, you drain on kitchen paper before serving with the sauce.

Spicy Mushroom Stir-Fry

Ingredients

1 teaspoon of whole brown mustard seeds

20 fresh basil leaves (torn)

2 clove garlic (sliced)

4-6 teaspoons of lime (or lemon juice)

6 tablespoons of extra virgin olive oil

½ teaspoon of whole fennel seeds

2 pound of cremini (or plain white mushrooms, sliced)

½ teaspoon of fine sea salt (to taste)

¼ teaspoon of cayenne pepper

Directions

1. First, you heat the olive oil in a large frying pan over medium-high heat.
2. After which you add in the mustard seeds and heat them for just a few seconds until they start to pop.
3. After that, you add in the fennel seeds and basil.
4. At this point, you stir for about 30 seconds, and add in the mushrooms and garlic.
5. Then you continue to stir, cooking the mixture for a few more minutes until mushrooms begin to lose their liquid.
6. Furthermore, you add in the salt, cayenne pepper and the lime juice, and stir for another minute or so.
7. Finally, you taste and adjust seasonings to suit your preference.
8. Then plate, serve and enjoy!

Hearty Lentil Soup with Tomatoes

Ingredients

2 onions (finely chopped)

4 carrots (chopped)

2 teaspoon of dried oregano

1 teaspoon of cayenne pepper (or to taste)

2 cans of diced tomatoes (including liquid)

2 pinch each of sea salt and freshly ground pepper (to taste)

2 tablespoons of extra virgin olive oil

2 celery stalk (chopped)

2 teaspoons of dried thyme

1 teaspoon of paprika

2 cups of lentils (rinsed)

8 cups of vegetable stock

Directions

1. First, you heat the olive oil in a large soup pot and add the onions.
2. After which you cook them for about 5 minutes or until they turn translucent.
3. After that, you add in the celery and carrots, and cook another 5 minutes or until they soften.
4. Then you add in the oregano, thyme, paprika and cayenne pepper along with the lentils, and stir until lentils and vegetables are coated with the spices.
5. Furthermore, you add the tomatoes and vegetable stock.

6. After that, you heat the soup to boiling, then reduce the heat and allow the soup to simmer for about 25-30 minutes until the lentils are cooked through.
7. At this point, you use an immersion blender, or in batches in a blender, blend the soup so that it is smoother, but still contains chunks of vegetables.
8. Finally, you ladle the hot soup into bowls, serve, and enjoy!

Hot and Spicy Curried Tofu Scramble

Ingredients

2 small onions (peeled and chopped)

2 teaspoons of ground coriander

2 teaspoons of fennel seeds

2 squeeze lemon juice (about 4 teaspoons)

24 oz. firm tofu (cubed)

2 teaspoons of ground cumin

2 teaspoons of dried chili flakes

2 teaspoons of ground turmeric

2 bag washed baby spinach leaves

Directions

1. First, you heat one tablespoon of olive oil in a large frying pan over medium-high heat.
2. After which you add the chopped onion and cook until it is just translucent.
3. After that, you add the spices and stir to coat the onions.
4. Then you cook together for about 30 seconds until the mixture is fragrant, then add the cubed tofu.
5. At this point, you gently stir everything together until it is thoroughly mixed.
6. This is when you cover the pan and cook for about 2-3 minutes, stirring occasionally, until the tofu is hot all the way through.

7. Furthermore, you add spinach and stir until the greens just barely begin to wilt, then add your lemon juice and stir as the spinach finishes wilting, about 10-15 seconds (NOTE: Be careful not to overcook the spinach).
8. Finally, you plate and serve the dish immediately, and enjoy a hot and spicy breakfast!

Spicy Roasted Cauliflower with Lemon

Ingredients:

Olive oil

4 tablespoons of lemon juice

Zest of 2 lemon

4 tablespoons of finely chopped parsley

2 head cauliflower, cut into stemmed florets (about 8 cups)

Kosher salt and freshly ground black pepper

2 teaspoons of honey (preferably use agave nectar for the vegan version)

2 teaspoons of crushed red pepper flakes

Directions:

1. Meanwhile, you heat the oven to a temperature of 450°F.
2. After which you toss the florets in a large bowl with a tablespoon or so of the olive oil, and season generously with salt and pepper.
3. After that, you grease a jelly roll-style cookie sheet (or preferably shallow roasting pan) with a bit more olive oil.
4. Then you spread the florets out in one layer on the prepared pan.
5. At this point, you roast the cauliflower for about 30-45 minutes, until it is cooked through and dark brown - even black - in most spots.
6. Meanwhile, you whisk together the lemon juice, honey and a pinch of salt in a small bowl.
7. Furthermore, you whisk in a tablespoon of oil and set aside.
8. Then once the cauliflower is roasted to your liking, you remove the pan from the oven and place the cooked cauliflower in a large bowl.
9. After which you toss with the lemon zest, crushed red pepper, parsley and a pinch of salt.

10. Finally, you mix well, taste and adjust for seasonings, and serve warm or at room temperature.

Carrot and celeriac root salad with lemon sauce [Vegan]
Ingredients:

3 largish carrots (cut into 3/4" slices)

Juice of 2 lemons

Salt and pepper (to taste)

4 tablespoons of extra-virgin olive oil
1 celeriac (weighing about 1 ¼ lbs.)
2 teaspoons of sugar

2 tablespoons of copped flat-leaf parsley

Directions:
1. First, you put the carrots and celeriac in a pan with just enough water to cover.
2. After which you add lemon, sugar and a little salt and pepper.
3. After that, you simmer for about 25-30 minutes, or until very tender, covering with the lid only part of the time, to reduce the liquid to a sauce.
4. Then you serve cold, dressed with olive oil and sprinkled with parsley.

Hearty Vegetable Soup with Pasta Shells

Ingredients

2 onion (chopped)

2 celery rib (sliced)

2 cups of tomato pasta sauce

2 pinch fine sea salt and freshly ground pepper, to taste

2 tablespoons of extra virgin olive oil

4 carrots (sliced)

12 mushrooms (sliced)

10 cups of vegetable stock

1 cup of small pasta shells

Directions

1. First, you heat the olive oil in a large pot, and add in the onions, carrots and celery.
2. After which you cook the vegetables for about 10 minutes until the onions are translucent.
3. After that, you add the mushrooms and cook until they have started to soften.
4. Then you add pasta sauce and vegetable stock and bring the pot to a simmer.
5. At this point, you continue to simmer for another 5 minutes or so, until the vegetables are almost tender.
6. Furthermore, you add pasta shells, and simmer until they are al dente.
7. After which, you give the soup a taste and add salt and pepper as needed.
8. Finally, you ladle soup into bowls, and enjoy!

Cucumber Salad with Honey-Lime Yogurt Dressing

Ingredients

1 cup of thinly sliced scallions (using just the white and light green parts)

4 tablespoons of chopped fresh mint

8 teaspoons of fresh-squeezed lime juice

½ teaspoon of ground coriander

4 tablespoons of toasted pine nuts for garnish

4 medium cucumbers

1 ½ cups of Greek-style yogurt

½ teaspoon of finely grated lime zest

4 teaspoons of honey

½ teaspoon of salt

Directions

1. First, you trim the ends off the cucumbers and peel them.
2. After which you slice them lengthwise then use a spoon to scoop the seeds out.
3. After that, you slice them into thin half-moons, and combine them with the sliced scallions into a mixing bowl.
4. Then you combine in a small bowl the yogurt, lime juice, mint, lime zest, honey, coriander and salt.
5. At this point, you whisk until thoroughly mixed.
6. Furthermore, you pour over the cucumber mix and stir to combine.
7. After which you spoon into bowls, and garnish with mint leaves and pine nuts.
8. Enjoy!

Swiss chard and Goat Cheese Casserole

Ingredients

4 tablespoons of extra virgin olive oil

4 cloves garlic (minced)

4 cups of whole wheat pasta shells

1 cup of canned kidney beans (drained and rinsed)

6 tablespoons of capers

2 pinches of freshly ground black pepper

2 large bunch Swiss chard (roughly chopped)

2 medium yellow onion (chopped)

2 cans of diced tomatoes (drained)

1 ½ cups of crumbled goat cheese

6 tablespoons of olive tapenade

½ cup of freshly grated Parmesan

Directions

1. Meanwhile, you heat the oven to a temperature of 375 degrees Fahrenheit.
2. After which you bring 4-5 cups of water in a large pot to a boil.
3. After that, you add in the pasta noodles and cook them until they're al dente.
4. This is when you drain them, and stir in a tiny bit of olive oil to keep them from sticking, set aside.
5. Then you heat the olive oil in a large heavy skillet over medium heat, and add the onions.

Quick Homemade Gluten

Ingredients:

2 teaspoons of garlic powder

2-1/2 cups of water or better still vegetable stock

2-6 teaspoons of toasted sesame oil (it is optional)

4 cups of gluten flour

2 teaspoons of ground ginger

6 Tablespoons lite tamari, Bragg's liquid amino acids, or soy sauce

Directions:

1. First, you add garlic powder and ginger to flour and stir.
2. After which you mix liquids together and add to flour mixture all at once.
3. After that, you mix vigorously with a fork.
4. Then when it forms a stiff dough knead it for 10 to 15 times.
5. At this point, you let the dough rest for about 2 to 5 minutes, then knead it a few more times.
6. Furthermore, you let it rest another 15 minutes before proceeding.
7. Finally, you cut gluten into 6 to 8 pieces and stretch into thin cutlets.
8. After which you simmer in broth for 30 to 60 minutes.

Seitan and Shiitake Mushroom Stroganoff

ingredients:

2 Tablespoons of oil

16-24 ounces of seitan cutlets (cut into chunks)

2 clove garlic (minced)

12 to 20 dried or fresh shiitake mushrooms (note: If dried they need to be soaked for at least 30 minutes and then drained.), sliced

10 ounces silken lite firm (or preferably extra firm tofu)

2 Tablespoons of arrowroot

½ cup of chopped parsley (for garnish Vegetable cooking spray)

2 onion (chopped)

2 carrots (finely cut or shredded)

2 cups of sliced button mushrooms

2 Tablespoons of Bragg liquid amino acids, lite tamari, or soy sauce

2 Tablespoons of lemon juice

2 teaspoons of sweetener

Freshly ground pepper (to taste)

Directions:
1. First, you spray a wok or large sauté pan with cooking spray.
2. After which you add the oil and heat.
3. Then when the oil is hot, you add the onion and seitan and sauté for 2 to 3 minutes.
4. After that, you add the carrot, garlic, and mushrooms.
5. This is when you cook until mushrooms release their water.

6. Furthermore, you add liquid aminos and cook until almost all absorbed.
7. At this point, while the mushroom mixture is cooking blend the tofu, lemon juice, arrowroot, and sweetener in a blender or food processor until smooth.
8. After that, you turn off heat and add the tofu mixture.
9. Then you stir to combine, but if heat is too high the tofu mixture will break apart and curdle.
10. In addition, you add freshly ground pepper.
11. Finally, you top with parsley and serve over hot noodles.

Seitan Fusion Sauté

ingredients:

2 medium onions (chopped)

2 Tablespoons of garam masala

4 cups of shredded zucchini

2-1 teaspoons of oil

4 cloves garlic (minced)

2 (8 ounces) seitan (finely chopped or coarsely grated)

2 cups of chopped fresh tomato

4 Tablespoons of peanut butter

Salt and pepper (to taste)

Dash of Tabasco (it is optional)

1 can crushed pineapple in juice, undrained (40 ounce can)

1 cup of lite coconut milk

½ cup of chopped fresh cilantro

Chopped peanuts for garnish (it is optional)

Directions:

1. First, you heat the oil in a large skillet.
2. After which you add the onion and sauté for about 5 minutes.
3. After that, you add the garlic and garam masala.
4. Then stirring, cook for another 1 to 2 minutes.
5. At this point, you add the zucchini, seitan, and tomato and cook for 1 to 2 minutes.

6. Furthermore, you add the remaining ingredients, except cilantro and simmer over medium heat for 10 minutes until sauce begins to thicken slightly.
7. This is when you taste and add Tabasco if desired.
8. After that, you stir in cilantro.
9. Finally, you top with chopped peanuts.
10. Make sure you serve hot over rice.

Barbecued Seitan

ingredients:

2 medium onion (diced)
8 whole wheat buns (it is optional)

Vegetable cooking spray

16-24 ounces seitan cutlets (cut into strips)
½ cup of barbecue sauce

Directions:

1. First, you spray a skillet with cooking spray.
2. After which you add the onion and sauté over medium heat for about 5 minutes, adding water 2 tablespoon at a time if onion begins to stick.
3. After that, you cook until onion is translucent.
4. Then you add the seitan strips and sauté for about 1 to 2 minutes.
5. Furthermore, you add barbecue sauce and stir to combine.
6. This is when you sauté until barbecue sauce is hot.
7. Finally, you serve on whole wheat buns, if you wish.

Seitan-Squash Sauté

ingredients:

2 medium onion (sliced)

1 pound of seitan, marinated in tamari broth (cut in small chunks)

2 medium-size zucchini (diced)

4 cloves garlic (minced)

1 cup of pineapple juice

4 teaspoons of vegetable oil

4 small carrots (peeled and sliced on the diagonal)

2 medium-size yellow squash (diced)

2 gray or roly-poly squash (diced)

2 teaspoons of grated ginger

2 large tomato (pureed)

2 Tablespoons of seitan marinade (or preferably 4 teaspoons tamari with 2 teaspoon water)
2 Tablespoons of arrowroot (starch) mixed with 2 tablespoon water

Directions:
1. First, you eat oil in large sauté pan over medium-high heat.
2. After which you add onion and carrots.
3. After that, you cook for about 5 minutes until onion starts getting translucent.
4. Then you add seitan, squash, garlic, and ginger and sauté for about 5 more minutes.
5. Furthermore, you add the pineapple juice, pureed tomato, and marinade.

6. At this point, you stir and cook for a couple of minutes.
7. This is when you remove pan from heat.
8. After that, you add the arrowroot mixture, stir well.
9. Finally, you return to heat and stir until sauce thickens.
10. Make sure you serve hot over rice or noodles.

Mock BBQ Pork

ingredients:

2 Tablespoons of toasted sesame oil

4 Tablespoons of water

2 Tablespoons of minced garlic

2 (8 ounces) gluten, cooked according to directions below

4 Tablespoons of lite tamari or soy sauce

2 Tablespoons of minced ginger

2 Tablespoons of sweetener

4 teaspoons of five-spice powder

Vegetable cooking spray

Directions:

1. First, you form gluten into a cylinder and lightly simmer in water for at least 30 minutes until quite firm.
2. After which you let cool and cut in small pieces in the Chinese "roll-cut" style. (Cut off one corner, turn the cylinder, cut again and continue.)
3. After that, you combine the remaining ingredients to make a marinade.
4. Then you marinate the gluten pieces for about 15 to 30 minutes.
5. Meanwhile, you heat the oven to 300 degrees.
6. At this point, you spray a baking sheet with cooking spray.
7. Furthermore, you drain gluten from marinade.
8. After that, you put on baking sheet and bake for about 20 to 30 minutes.

NOTE: if gluten seems to be getting too dry, I suggest you baste with the marinade.

CONCLUSION

These 22 DAY VEGAN CHALLENGE would help you Shred the Fat Instantly and keep the weight off for good. Get in shape and live a healthier lifestyle this Season taking these vegan smoothie recipes. If you follow religiously to the "22 Day Revolution" By Marco Borges and some of the recipes outlined in this book. You are going to be seeing results in 22 days, because it is proven to work.

VEGAN REV' DEIT RECIPES

www.ingramcontent.com/pod-product-compliance
Lightning Source LLC
Chambersburg PA
CBHW081728100526
44591CB00016B/2544